For the love of my life.
Always alive in my heart.
NBR

"And among His signs is this, that He created for you mates from among your-
selves, that ye may dwell in tranquility with them, and He has put love and
mercy between your (hearts). Verily in that are signs for those who reflect."

Verse 30:21, Chapter ar-Rum, Holy Qur'an

JANETTA OTTER-BARRY BOOKS

Text copyright © Na'ima B Robert 2016
Illustrations copyright © Shirin Adl 2016

The rights of Na'ima B Robert and Shirin Adl to be identified as the author and illustrator
of this work have been asserted by them in accordance with the Copyright,
Designs and Patents Act, 1988 (United Kingdom).
First published in Great Britain and in the USA in 2016 by
Frances Lincoln Children's Books, 74-77 White Lion Street, London N1 9PF
www.franceslincoln.com

A catalogue record for this book is available from the British Library.

ISBN 978-1-84780-588-1

Illustrated with acrylic and collage

Printed in China

1 3 5 7 9 8 6 4 2

MaBROOK!

A World of Muslim Weddings

Written by
Na'ima B Robert

Illustrated by
Shirin Adl

Frances Lincoln
Children's Books

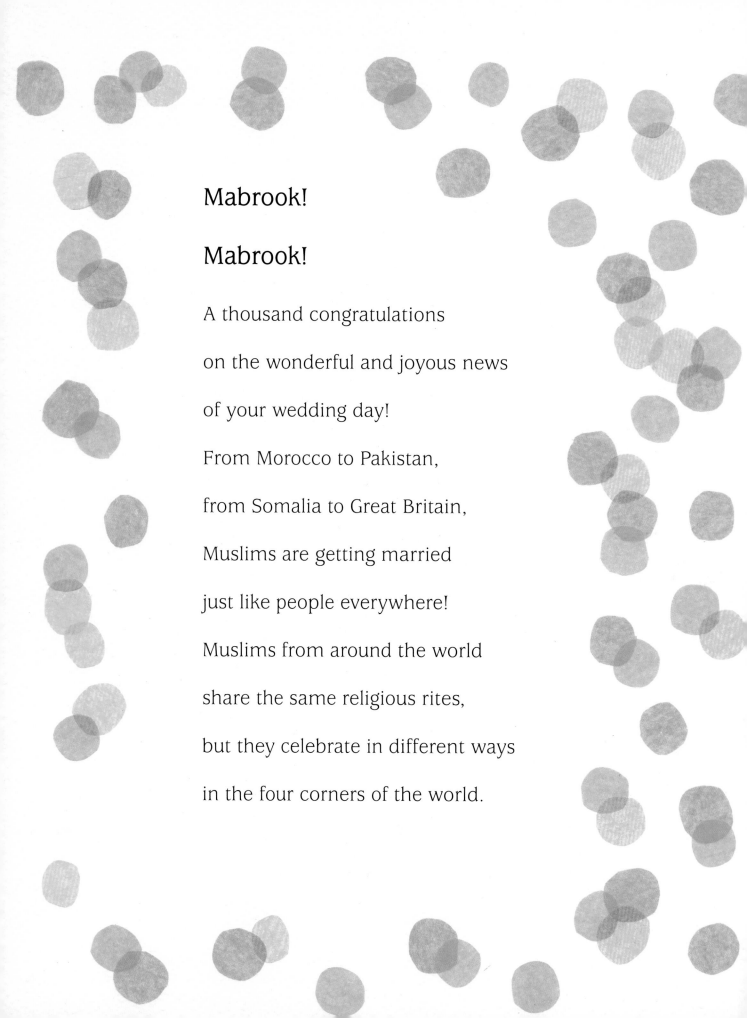

Mabrook!

Mabrook!

A thousand congratulations

on the wonderful and joyous news

of your wedding day!

From Morocco to Pakistan,

from Somalia to Great Britain,

Muslims are getting married

just like people everywhere!

Muslims from around the world

share the same religious rites,

but they celebrate in different ways

in the four corners of the world.

In Pakistan

there's a henna party

before the wedding day,

for the bride and her mother,

her sisters and aunties,

her cousins, family and friends.

Henna patterns adorn hands and feet,

to make her a gorgeous bride.

On the day, the groom rides in

on a great white horse.

His bride hides under silk and henna

and lots

and lots

of gold.

Girls in shiny sandals and armfuls of bangles

run between the tables

of *biryani* and *rasmalai*.

And all the guests

from far and wide

say prayers for the bride and groom.

In Morocco

a wedding is a community affair.

All the neighbours cook together

for days

and days

and days.

Couscous and roasted lamb

with olives and pickled lemons,

enough to feed the multitudes

who will attend the feast.

At the *waleemah* the bride is beautiful,

carried in above the crowd.

Each time she looks more elegant

as she changes seven times.

Shrill cries of joy pierce the air

as she dances in the circle of song.

In Somalia

no wedding is complete

without the *buraanbur*.

The older ladies lead the dance

while the young girls clap and sing.

Their *diracs* flow and sweep the ground,

the drum throbs with a rhythmic sound,

and the women sing

for God's blessings

on the mother of the bride.

In Britain,

in a scented garden,

the bride wears a white *hijab*.

She is surrounded by her sisters in faith

from all around the world.

There is wedding cake and biryani,

hijabs, kilts and *kurtas*.

The *imam* has a great big ginger beard

and the best man gives a speech.

The couple's guests are a wonderful mix

of different backgrounds, different faiths,

all there to witness and celebrate

the start of a new love story.

And though Muslims celebrate in different ways

all around the world,

they all share the same ceremonies,

the same religious rites.

Before the party,

before the presents,

before the fanfare, food, and fun,

there are noble intentions,

family meetings

and important conversations.

There is an agreement,

a marriage contract,

conditions to be respected,

guidance that is sought

for the union to be blessed.

The groom pledges his gift – the *mahr*,

a dowry for his bride.

It may be gold, a ring, a house, or *Hajj*,

or whatever her heart desires.

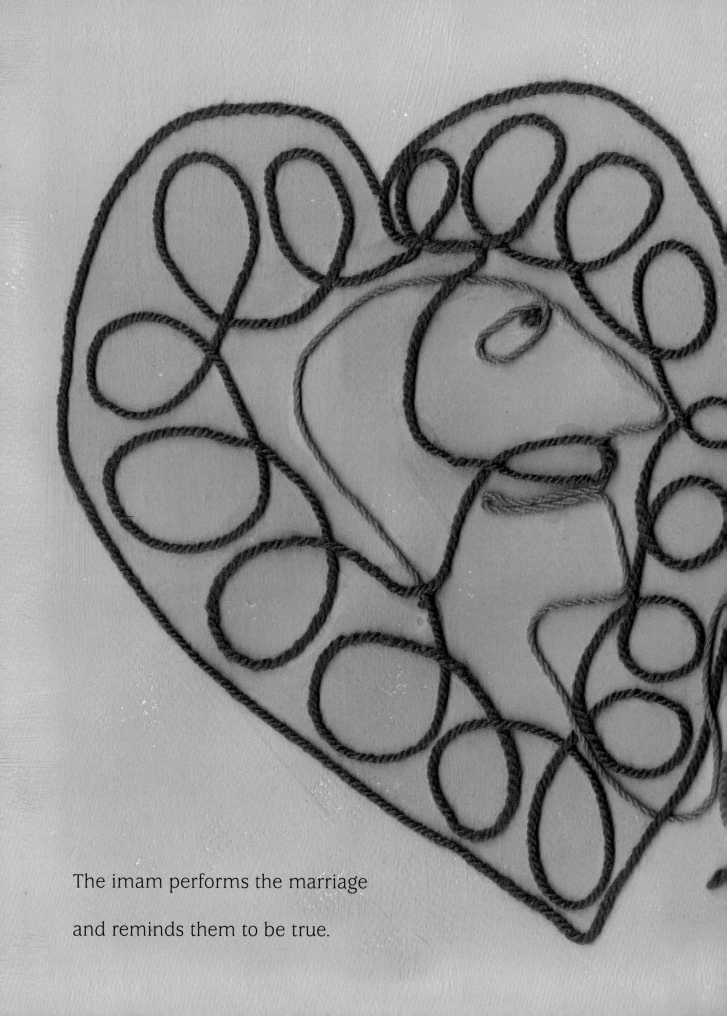

The imam performs the marriage

and reminds them to be true.

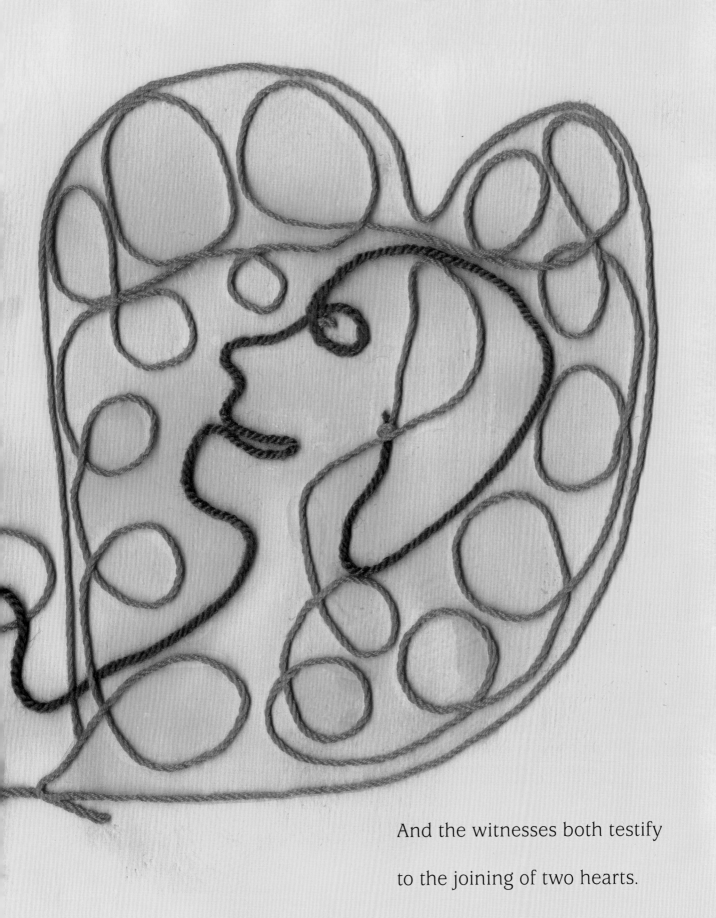

And the witnesses both testify

to the joining of two hearts.

For after the wedding is over,

after the hall is bare,

after the gold has been put away

and food has been sent out to share,

when the last guest has departed

and the last song has been sung,

the happy couple ride off together.

Their new journey has begun.

Mabrook!

About Muslim Weddings

In the Muslim community, weddings are truly something to celebrate. They represent continuity, tradition and the union of two people, two families. There is a poignant mixture of anticipation, excitement and a good dose of nerves! I wanted to write a book about how Muslim weddings are celebrated in different parts of the world to illustrate our similarities and our differences, both within the Muslim community and within the context of the wider global community. I hope you've enjoyed the tour.

   Na'ima B Robert

Glossary

biryani: a spicy rice dish popular in India and Pakistan

buraanbur: traditional Somali dance

dirac: traditional Somali dress

Hajj: the pilgrimage to Mecca

hijab: the headscarf or covering worn by Muslim women

imam: a Muslim religious leader

kurta: a traditional Pakistani or Indian tunic

mabrook: congratulations

mahr: the gift that the groom gives the bride

rasmalai: a sweet, milky, Bengali dessert often served at weddings

waleemah: the wedding feast to which the community is invited